U.S.A.
SECRET CODE
PUZZLES
FOR KIDS

Tony J. Tallarico

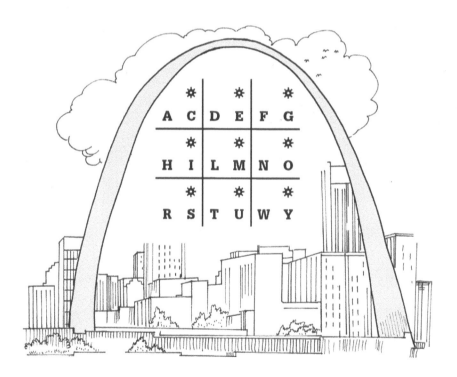

Dover Publications
Garden City, New York

Note

The dozens of activities in this fun-filled puzzle book will keep you challenged and entertained from start to finish. Using codes of various sorts, crosswords, word searches, and other cleverly designed activities, you'll learn facts about the United States as you enjoy solving the puzzles. Answer questions such as "What does E Pluribus Unum" mean?," "What does the 'D.C.' in 'Washington, D.C.' stand for?," and "Why was the U.S. Secret Service first created?" American presidents, U.S. historical events, and fun facts all play a part in this unique collection.

Copyright

Copyright © 2014 by Tony J. Tallarico
All rights reserved.

Bibliographical Note

U.S.A. Secret Code Puzzles for Kids is a new work, first published by Dover Publications in 2014. ᶦ.

International Standard Book Number

ISBN-13: 978-0-486-49459-3
ISBN-10: 0-486-49459-4

Manufactured in the United States of America
ScoutAutomatedPrintCode
www.doverpublications.com

Alaska's Coastlines

Alaska is the only state to have coastlines on three different bodies of water. What are they?
Use the chart below to decode the answer.

	A	B	C	D	E
1	R	N	D	H	F
2	T	I	B	G	O
3	C	E	A	P	S

2A 1D 3B   3C 1A 3A 2A 2B 3A

2E 3A 3B 3C 1B '   2A 1D 3B

3D 3C 3A 2B 1E 2B 3A

2E 3A 3B 3C 1B   3C 1B 1C   2A 1D 3B

2C 3B 1A 2B 1B 2D   3E 3B 3C

Cereal Bowl Of America

This U.S. location is known as the "Cereal Bowl of America," because it produces more breakfast cereal than anywhere else in the world.

What is the name of this Michigan city?

Write these 11 words in alphabetical order into the puzzle grid. The fourth letter of each word will help spell out the answer.

SWEEP

MARCH

JOLLY

BRIBE

SPORT

CLEAN

STEED

WORKS

HASTE

LIVED

DARTS

Cooking Mistake

A simple cooking error by Ruth Wakefield, who ran a Massachusetts inn, led to what famous treat?
Write the names of these desserts in their correct spaces.
Then use the numbered letters to decode and complete the answer below.

**CAKE
CUPCAKE
ICE CREAM
LICORICE
PASTRY
PUDDING**

$$\underline{\hphantom{X}}\ \underline{\hphantom{X}}\ \underline{\text{T}}\ \underline{\hphantom{X}}\ \underline{\text{É}}\ \underline{\hphantom{X}}\ \underline{\text{L}}\ \underline{\text{L}}$$
$$\ \ 1\ \ \ 2\ \ \ 3\ \ \ \ \ 4\ \ \ \ \ \ 5\ \ \ 6$$

$$\underline{\text{H}}\ \underline{\text{O}}\ \underline{\hphantom{X}}\ \underline{\text{S}}\ \underline{\hphantom{X}}\ \underline{\hphantom{X}}\ \underline{\text{H}}\ \underline{\text{O}}\ \underline{\hphantom{X}}\ \underline{\text{O}}\ \underline{\text{L}}\ \underline{\hphantom{X}}\ \underline{\text{T}}\ \underline{\hphantom{X}}$$
$$\ \ \ \ \ \ 7\ \ \ \ \ 8\ \ \ \ \ 9\ \ \ \ \ \ 10\ \ \ \ \ \ 11\ \ \ \ \ 12$$

$$\underline{\hphantom{X}}\ \underline{\text{H}}\ \underline{\hphantom{X}}\ \underline{\hphantom{X}}\ \underline{\hphantom{X}}\ \underline{\text{O}}\ \underline{\text{O}}\ \underline{\hphantom{X}}\ \underline{\hphantom{X}}\ \underline{\hphantom{X}}$$
$$\ \ 13\ \ \ \ 14\ 15\ \ \ \ \ 16\ \ \ \ \ \ \ 17\ 18\ 19$$

3

Early To Bed, Early To Rise

Who said "Early to bed, early to rise, makes a man healthy, wealthy and wise"?

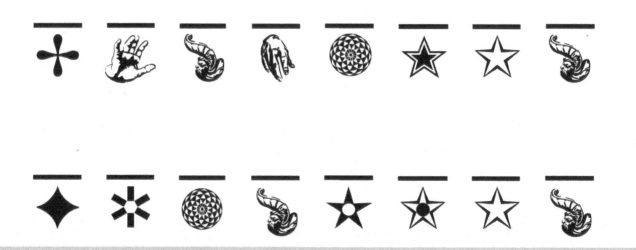

E Pluribus Unum

The inscription "E Pluribus Unum" printed on U.S. bills and coins was first used on the gold $5 piece back in 1795. What does E Pluribus Unum mean? Write the names of these objects in their spaces to the right. Then place the numbered letters in the correct spaces below to decode and complete the answer.

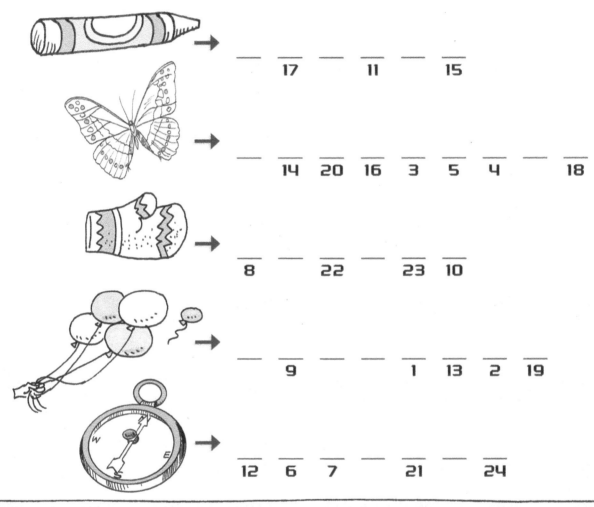

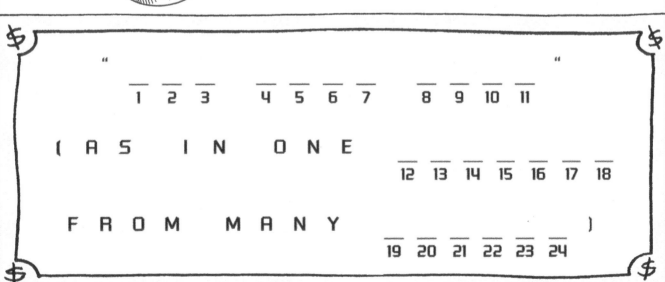

First Lady Landscaping

The planting of cherry blossom trees in Washington, D.C., originated as a gift to the U.S. from Japan.
In March 1912, one of the first two flowering cherry trees to grace our nation's capital was planted by a president's wife. Today there are more than 3,700 cherry trees in Washington, D.C., including the one this First Lady planted!

1	2	3	4	5	6	7	8	9	10	11
E	K	P	G	M	R	C	S	O	I	Y

12	13	14	15	16	17	18	19	20	21	22
H	V	A	W	U	F	T	N	D	L	B

"
12 1 21 1 19   19 1 21 21 10 1

"
18 14 17 18 , W I F E O F

P R E S I D E N T

15 10 21 21 10 14 5

12 9 15 14 6 20

18 14 17 18 .

Flying Out of Town

Although they were based in Ohio, why did Orville and Wilbur Wright bring their flying machine to Kitty Hawk, North Carolina? Crack this code by writing the letter of the alphabet that comes BEFORE each letter.

U I F   O B U J P O B M

X F B U I F S   T F S W J D F

S F Q P S U F E   U I B U

J U   X B T   P O F   P G

U I F   X J O E J F T U

T Q P U T   J O   O P S U I

B N F S J D B .

For Sale

A website known as AuctionWeb first launched during Labor Day Weekend 1995. Today we know the site as eBay. What was the first item ever listed? Use this special code to decipher the answer.

A	B	C
D	E	I
K	L	M

N	O	P
Q	R	S
T	U	Y

Largest Privately Owned U.S. Home

Built between 1889 and 1895 by George Washington Vanderbilt II, this French château-style mansion with 250 rooms is the largest privately owned home in the U.S. What is the name of this home and where is it located? Crack this code by writing the letter of the alphabet that comes BEFORE each letter.

THAT IS SOME NEST!

U I F   C J M U N P S F

F T U B U F   O F B S

B T I F W J M M F ,

O P S U I

D B S P M J O B

9

Lincoln's Tomb

Abraham Lincoln is not buried in the Lincoln Memorial.
Where is our 16th president's tomb located?
Decode the answer using this special code chart.

❀	D
◨	I
◇	P
❋	N
⊞	S
⊠	R
⊠	I
◈	G
❁	L
◉	O
⣿	E
⊞	S
✿	I
❀	L
❋	N
◎	I
✳	F
❀	L
✠	I

Microwave Oven

How was the microwave oven accidentally invented?
Cross out all the odd-numbered letters in this puzzle grid. List the remaining letters, in the order they appear, in the spaces below.

14	6	2	13	17	22	5	4	18	21	8	41	1
A	R	E	T	I	S	U	E	A	W	R	Y	E
10	24	1	12	45	16	11	14	71	4	10	26	71
C	H	Q	E	V	R	A	W	E	A	L	K	D
13	3	57	30	18	11	20	25	2	17	14	32	11	53	12
E	H	M	E	D	N	B	O	Y	T	A	R	G	N	A
4	5	28	14	81	2	11	8	34	22	1	44	6	38	11
D	Q	A	R	I	T	A	U	B	E	M	A	N	D	B
7	10	16	37	54	34	14	47	64	4	12	19	14	74	81
H	A	C	S	H	O	C	T	O	L	A	D	T	E	Z
83	11	2	60	21	52	51	14	4	3	6	22	56	5	3
Y	F	B	A	W	R	S	I	N	S	H	I	S	Z	R
55	68	9	54	7	34	8	5	10	37	14	11	1	17	21
U	P	A	O	R	C	K	S	E	C	T	H	E	R	G
26	13	1	61	32	48	4	3	11	65	75	7	2	14	51
M	S	M	R	E	L	T	Y	A	I	O	U	E	D	Z

__ __ __ __ __ __ __ __ __ __

__ __ __ __ __ __ __ __ __

__ __ __ __ __ __ __ __ __

__ __ __ __ __

__ __ __ __ __ __

__ __ __ __ __ __ __ __ !

Miss Liberty's Crown

There are seven rays on the Statue of Liberty's crown, each measuring up to 9 feet in length and weighing as much as 150 pounds. What do the rays stand for? Decode the answer using the chart below.

A	●-	J	●---	S	●●●
B	-●●●	K	-●-	T	-
C	-●-●	L	●-●●	U	●●-
D	-●●	M	--	V	●●●-
E	●	N	-●	W	●--
F	●●-●	O	---	X	-●●-
G	--●	P	●--●	Y	-●--
H	●●●●	Q	--●-	Z	--●●
I	●●	R	●-●		

_ _ _
\- ●●●● ●

_ _ _ _ _
●●● ● ●●●- ● -●

_ _ _ _ _ _ _ _ _ _
-●-● --- -● - ●● -● ● -● - ●●●

Mother, Wife & Cousin

Name the only person to be a mother, wife, and cousin to a U.S. President.

As you read each sentence below, decide whether the statement is true or false.

If the sentence is true, circle the letter under the TRUE column. If the sentence is false, circle the letter under the FALSE column. The circled letters, once listed below in the order they appear, will reveal the answer.

	TRUE	FALSE
1. The city of Paris is located in France.	B	A
2. Valentine's Day is celebrated on February 14.	A	E
3. The first man walked on the moon in 1999.	C	R
4. George Washington had a pet dinosaur.	I	B
5. Albert Einstein owned the first Apple computer.	L	A
6. Bananas contain potassium.	R	O
7. Frogs can give you warts.	S	A
8. There are 30 days in November.	B	T
9. Benjamin Franklin invented bifocals.	U	R
10. Dragons existed during the Middle Ages.	E	S
11. Twelve inches equal one foot.	H	Y

— — — — — — — — — — — —

No Election

This is the only man who held both the Presidency and the Vice-Presidency but who was not elected to either post. Discover his name by first drawing a line through these presidential words hidden in the puzzle below.
The letters that remain in the puzzle, once listed in the order they appear, will spell out the answer.

ADVISORS
CABINET
CAPITOL
CONGRESS
DEMOCRAT
LIMIT
OATH
OFFICE
REPUBLICAN
SENATE
STAFF
TERM

N A C I L B U P E R

O D E M O C R A T F F

F V E G H E R A E F

F I T T L D F O R A

I S A L I M I T M T

C O N G R E S S R S

E R E T E N I B A C

D S S L O T I P A C

— — — — — — — — — — — — —

Now Hiring

What U.S. company currently employs more than 2 million people, making it the largest employer in America?
Darken in the areas that have a DOT ● to discover the answer.

Of Monumental Size

Opened in 1967 and standing 630 feet tall, this is the tallest man-made monument in the United States. Solve the secret code to find out what this is and where it can be found.

Our Nation's Capital

Washington, D.C. is not a state. Named after President George Washington, what does the D.C. stand for? Decode and complete the answer.

A	B	C	D	E	F	G	H	I	L
ny	ca	fl	nj	ct	vt	tx	nd	va	al

M	N	O	P	R	S	T	U	V	Y
co	ks	nv	ut	wy	ak	az	de	ga	ma

D I S T R I C T   O F
nj va ak az wy va fl az   nv vt

C O L U M B I A ,
fl nv al de co ca va ny

"DISTRICT" BECAUSE IT IS NOT PART OF A

S T A T E   A N D
ak az ny az ct   ny ks nj

"COLUMBIA" FOR

N A V I G A T O R
ks ny ga va tx ny az nv wy

C H R I S T O P H E R
fl nd wy va ak az nv ut nd ct wy

C O L U M B U S .
fl nv al de co ca de ak

Paul Revere's Midnight Ride

Paul Revere never shouted the legendary phrase "The British are coming!" In 1775, since colonists still considered themselves British, that would have been confusing. What do historians think is more likely that Revere told the other rebels? Decipher the code to find out.

Peanuts?

Most of us call the main ingredient in peanut butter ... peanuts.
But what do Georgia locals call them?
Write the name of each picture in its space. One letter from
each word will spell out the answer.

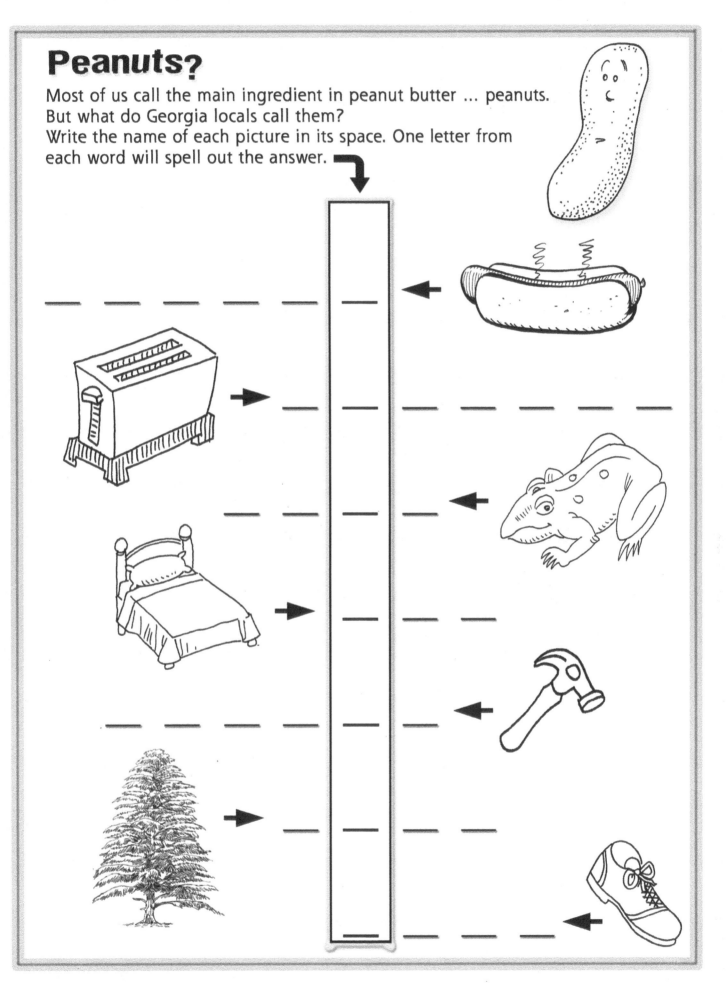

Pony Express

What state capital city was once the last stop for the Pony Express?
Decipher the code to find out.

Popular Children's Novel

What American novel, written by Louisa May Alcott, is about four sisters named Meg, Jo, Beth and Amy? Write the opposite of each word in the puzzle grid. One letter from each will spell out and decode the answer.

DROP __ __ __ __

TAKE __ __ __ __

STAND __ __ __

CATCH __ __ __ __ __

RIGHT __ __ __ __

TEACH __ __ __ __ __

STRONG __ __ __ __

SUNNY __ __ __ __ __

WOMAN __ __ __

ENTER __ __ __ __

BEGIN __ __ __

Presidential Portraits

Celebrated artist Norman Rockwell is known for his patriotic illustrations of American life. Rockwell painted portraits of only 4 U.S. presidents. The word PORTRAIT appears 7 times in this puzzle. Find and circle each one. The letters that remain, once listed below in the order they appear, will spell out the names of these four presidents.

```
P O R T R A I T E
O I S E N H O P T
R W E R K E O N I
T I A R T R O P A
R N E D T Y J O R
A P O R T R A I T
I H A N S O N A R
T I A R T R O P O
T N D N I X O N P
```

— — — — — — — — — — ,

— — — — — — — — ,

— — — — — —

— — — — — — — —

President's Airplane

Name the airplane used by the President of the United States. As you read each sentence below, decide whether the statement is true or false. If the sentence is true, circle the letter under the TRUE column. If the sentence is false, circle the letter under the FALSE column. The circled letters, once listed below in the order they appear, will reveal the answer.

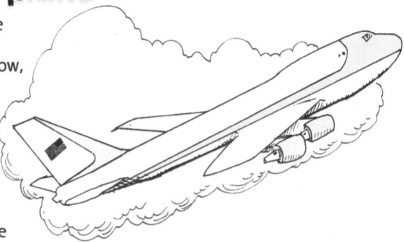

	TRUE	FALSE
1. Nine times five equals fourteen.	T	A
2. Mars is also known as the Red Planet.	I	O
3. Dolphins are intelligent animals.	R	E
4. Water covers 10% of the Earth's surface.	I	F
5. A Leap Year occurs every 25 years.	L	O
6. Astronomers study objects found in space.	R	Y
7. Red, blue and yellow are called the primary colors.	C	A
8. Thomas Jefferson invented the cellular phone.	B	E
9. Abe Lincoln was the tallest U.S. President.	O	U
10. The year is divided into 4 seasons.	N	S
11. Everyone in Alaska lives in igloos.	T	E

— — — — —   — — — — —   — — — — —

"Satchmo"

Known around the world as "Satchmo," this cultural icon is widely recognized as a founding father of jazz.
Who is this musician from New Orleans who helped make jazz famous with his trumpet and unique singing voice?

Secret Service

We think of the Secret Service as a group of agents that protect the President of the United States. But why was the U.S. Secret Service first created?

Solve this crossword puzzle. Then list the circled letters, in the order they appear, in the spaces below to form the answer.

ACROSS

1. Sports statue award
5. Water from the sky
6. Heavy jacket
7. Midday meal
9. Really great or awesome
11. Opposite of stand

DOWN

2. Halloween month
3. Where you live
4. Not big
8. Grown kittens
10. You stand on these
11. To vocalize musically

___ __ _____ ____ _____ _____

___ ____ __ _____ ____ ____ ___

Serving Others

A pioneer American teacher, patent clerk, nurse, and humanitarian, this woman from Massachusetts built a career helping others. Who was this founder of the American Red Cross?

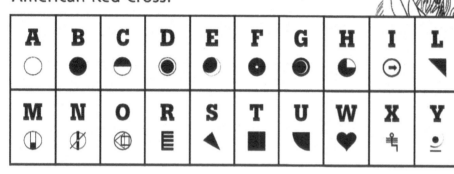

A Shocking Win

On August 24, 1919, Cleveland Indians pitcher Ray Caldwell completed a winning game against the Philadelphia Athletics. What was so unusual about this win? Cross out only the letters that contain this symbol ▦. The remaining letters, once listed below in the order they appear, will spell out the answer.

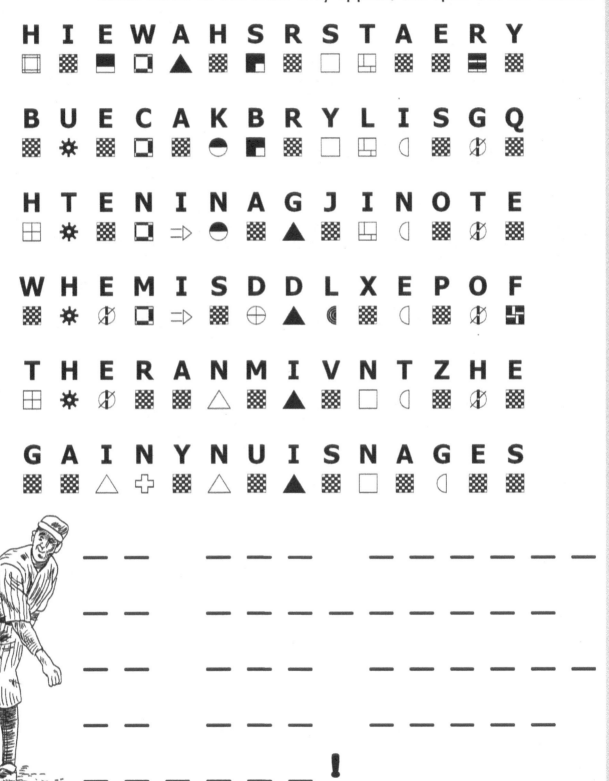

Answer: HE WAS STRUCK BY LIGHTNING IN THE MIDDLE OF THE NINTH INNING!

Shortest Inaugural Address

Did you know that George Washington gave the shortest inaugural address in history, all because of his painful dentures? He only had one real tooth left at the time of his second inaugural, and his speech consisted of only 135 words. How long did it take President Washington to deliver this speech? Circle all the even-numbered letters and list them, in the order they appear, in the blank spaces below.

5	9	12	7	4	1
T	E	N	A	I	S
2	**15**	**3**	**10**	**6**	**11**
N	B	R	E	T	P
9	**14**	**8**	**13**	**19**	**16**
C	Y	S	T	U	E
5	**1**	**2**	**20**	**17**	**5**
W	N	C	O	M	T
18	**25**	**3**	**4**	**21**	**12**
N	T	A	D	E	S

My dentures were not made of wood. As I was a wealthy man, I could afford dentures made of gold and ivory. But they still hurt!

‾ ‾ ‾ ‾ ‾ ‾ ‾

‾ ‾ ‾ ‾ ‾ ‾ ‾

Shortest Presidency

He gave the longest inaugural address in U.S. history, but had the shortest presidency. To decode his name, write the letter of the alphabet that comes BEFORE each letter.

X J M M J B N   I F O S Z

I B S S J T P O '

X I P

E J F E   K V T U

U I J S U Z   P O F

E B Z T   J O U P   I J T

U F S N   G S P N

Q O F V N P O J B

Soft Drink in Space

What was the first soft drink to be consumed in space?
Answer each clue correctly.
Then write the numbered letters in their correct spaces at the bottom of the page to decode and complete the answer.

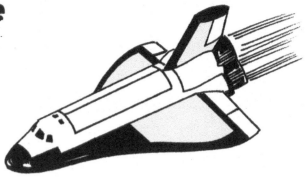

Clue	Answer
Tenth month of the year	O __ T __ B __ __ 9 2 14 18
Space traveler	__ S T R __ __ __ U T 4 6 15 8
Enclosed area to keep clothes in	__ __ O S __ T 1 7 17
Device used to tell time	__ __ O __ K 3 12 5
Not solid	__ O L __ O W 10 13
Small, medium and _____	L __ R __ E 11 16

__ __ __ __ - __ __ __ __
1 2 3 4   5 6 7 8

A B O A R D   T H E   S P A C E   S H U T T L E

__ __ __ __ __ __ __ __ __ __
9 10 11 12 13 14 15 16 17 18

Special Delivery

Where is the only place in the U.S. where
mail is still delivered by mule?

MAIL'S
HERE!

A	↰
B	⇄
C	↳
D	↔
E	↕
F	↔
G	↔
H	⇄
I	⇉
L	↷
M	↻
N	↪
O	↺
P	↻
R	↻
S	⤨
T	∧
U	↷
V	↺
Y	⇑

Sticky Candy

What sticky candy was invented at a New Jersey seashore in the 1870s?
Answer each clue correctly. Then write the numbered letters in their correct
spaces at the bottom of the page to decode the answer.

Opposite of slow	$\overline{12}\ \overline{6}\ \underline{\quad}\ \overline{4}$
Cold season	$\overline{5}\ \underline{\quad}\ \underline{\quad}\ \overline{7}\ \underline{\quad}\ \overline{9}$
Winged insect	$\overline{13}\ \overline{3}\ \overline{14}$
Morning meal	$\underline{\quad}\ \underline{\quad}\ \overline{8}\ \overline{2}\ \underline{\quad}\ \underline{\quad}\ \overline{11}\ \overline{1}\ \overline{10}$

$\overline{1}\quad \overline{2}\quad \overline{3}\quad \overline{4}\quad \overline{5}\quad \overline{6}\quad \overline{7}\quad \overline{8}\quad \overline{9}$

$\overline{10}\quad \overline{11}\quad \overline{12}\quad \overline{13}\quad \overline{14}$

Tallest Tree

Where is the tallest known tree on Earth and what type is it?
To decode the answer, cross out each letter that appears
SIX times in this puzzle grid. List the remaining letters,
in the order they appear, in the blank spaces below.

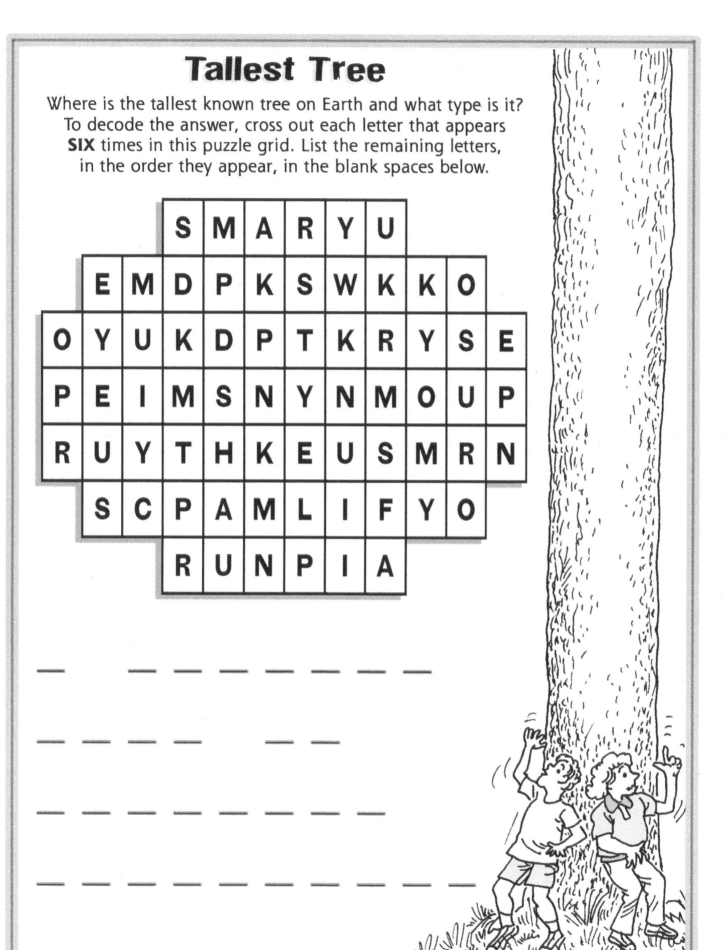

S	M	A	R	Y	U

E	M	D	P	K	S	W	K	K	O

O	Y	U	K	D	P	T	K	R	Y	S	E

P	E	I	M	S	N	Y	N	M	O	U	P

R	U	Y	T	H	K	E	U	S	M	R	N

S	C	P	A	M	L	I	F	Y	O

R	U	N	P	I	A

____ ____ ____ ____ ____ ____ ____ ____ ____ ____ ____

____ ____ ____ ____ ____ ____

____ ____ ____ ____ ____ ____ ____ ____ ____

____ ____ ____ ____ ____ ____ ____ ____ ____ ____ ____

33

Tennessee Tunes

What Tennessee city is known as "Music City, USA"? To decode the answer, first draw a line through these 7 musical words hidden in the puzzle below. The letters that remain in the puzzle, once listed in the order they appear, will spell out the answer.

BAND ● **BASS** ● **FIDDLE**

GUITAR ● **HARMONY** ● **PIANO** ● **SINGER**

N	A	S	R	A	T	I	U	G
H	V	I	L	L	E	R	T	F
H	E	H	O	O	M	E	E	I
O	F	C	N	O	U	G	D	D
N	H	A	R	M	O	N	Y	D
T	I	R	Y	M	A	I	U	L
P	S	I	C	B	A	S	S	E

___ ___ ___ ___ ___ ___ ___ ___ ___ ,

___ ___ ___ ___ ___ ___ ___ ___ ___

___ ___ ___ ___ ___ ___ ___ ___

___ ___ ___ ___ ___ ___

Thirteen Stripes

The American flag today consists of thirteen horizontal stripes.
What does the number 13 stand for?
Darken in the areas that have a DOT • to decode the answer.

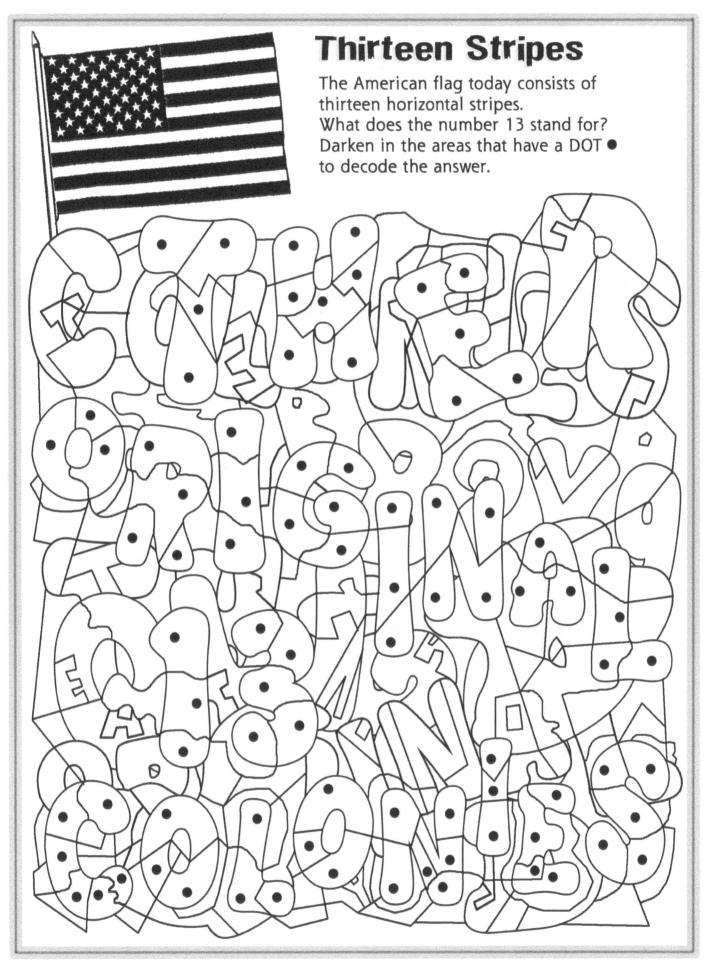

Wilderness Trail

What is the name of the wilderness trail that stretches from
Mount Katahdin in Maine all the way south to Springer Mountain in Georgia?
Use this special code to decipher the answer.

Solutions

Alaska's Coastlines

Alaska is the only state to have coastlines on three different bodies of water. What are they? Use the chart below to decode the answer.

	A	B	C	D	E
1	R	N	D	H	F
2	T	I	B	G	O
3	C	E	A	P	S

T H E · · A R C T I C
2A 1D 3B · · 3C 1A 3A 2A 2B 3A

O C E A N , · · T H E
2E 3A 3B 3C 1B · · 2A 1D 3B

P A C I F I C
3D 3C 3A 2B 1E 2B 3A

O C E A N · · A N D · · T H E
2E 3A 3B 3C 1B · · 3C 1B 1C · · 2A 1D 3B

B E R I N G · · S E A
2C 3B 1A 2B 1B 2D · · 3E 3B 3C

page 1

Cereal Bowl Of America

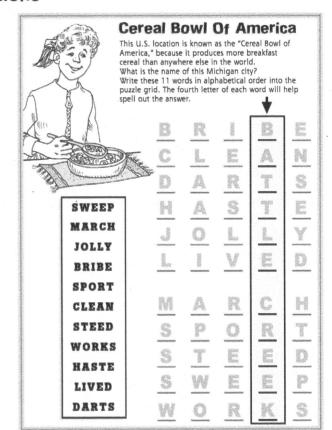

This U.S. location is known as the "Cereal Bowl of America," because it produces more breakfast cereal than anywhere else in the world. What is the name of this Michigan city? Write these 11 words in alphabetical order into the puzzle grid. The fourth letter of each word will help spell out the answer.

Word list:
SWEEP
MARCH
JOLLY
BRIBE
SPORT
CLEAN
STEED
WORKS
HASTE
LIVED
DARTS

Grid:
BRIBE
CLEAR
DARTS
HASTLE
JOLLY
LIVED
MARCH
SPORT
STEED
SWEEP
WORKS

(fourth letters spell: BATTLE CREEKS)

page 2

Cooking Mistake

A simple cooking error by Ruth Wakefield, who ran a Massachusetts inn, led to what famous treat? Write the names of these desserts in their correct spaces. Then use the numbered letters to decode and complete the answer below.

CAKE
CUPCAKE
ICE CREAM
LICORICE
PASTRY
PUDDING

Crossword answers: CUPCAKE, LICORICE, ICE CREAM, PASTRY, PUDDING, CAKE

N E S T L É · T O L L
1 2 3 · 4 · 5 6

H O U S E · C H O C O L A T E
· 7 8 · 9 · 10 · 11 12

C H I P · C O O K I E
13 14 15 · 16 · 17 18 19

page 3

Early To Bed, Early To Rise

Who said "Early to bed, early to rise, makes a man healthy, wealthy and wise"?

= A   ★ = M   = J
= E   ☆ = I
✛ = B   = N
◆ = F
                   ☆ = K
✳ = R   ★ = L

B E N J A M I N
✛ ✳ ... ... ★ ☆ ...

F R A N K L I N
◆ ✳ ... ... ☆ ★ ☆ ...

page 4

37

E Pluribus Unum

The inscription "E Pluribus Unum" printed on U.S. bills and coins was first used on the gold $5 piece back in 1795. What does E Pluribus Unum mean? Write the names of these objects in their spaces to the right. Then place the numbered letters in the correct spaces below to decode and complete the answer.

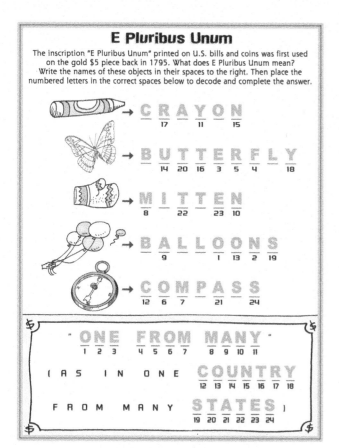

C R A Y O N
17 11 15

B U T T E R F L Y
14 20 16 3 5 4   18

M I T T E N
8   22 23 10

B A L L O O N S
9   1 13 2 19

C O M P A S S
12 7   21 24

"O N E   F R O M   M A N Y"
1 2 3   4 5 6 7   8 9 10 11

(A S   I N   O N E   C O U N T R Y
                       12 13 14 15 16 17 18

F R O M   M A N Y   S T A T E S)
                    19 20 21 22 23 24

First Lady Landscaping

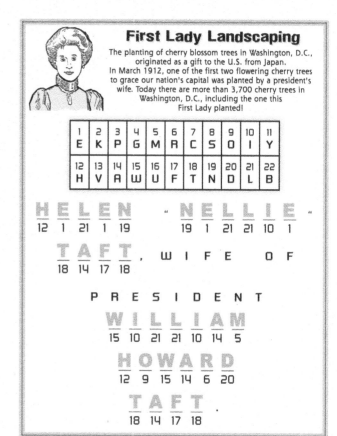

The planting of cherry blossom trees in Washington, D.C., originated as a gift to the U.S. from Japan. In March 1912, one of the first two flowering cherry trees to grace our nation's capital was planted by a president's wife. Today there are more than 3,700 cherry trees in Washington, D.C., including the one this First Lady planted!

1	2	3	4	5	6	7	8	9	10	11
E	K	P	G	M	R	C	S	O	I	Y

12	13	14	15	16	17	18	19	20	21	22
H	V	A	W	U	F	T	N	D	L	B

H E L E N   " N E L L I E "
12 1 21 1 19   19 1 21 21 10 1

T A F T,   W I F E   O F
18 14 17 18

P R E S I D E N T

W I L L I A M
15 10 21 21 10 14 5

H O W A R D
12 9 15 14 6 20

T A F T.
18 14 17 18

Flying Out of Town

Although they were based in Ohio, why did Orville and Wilbur Wright bring their flying machine to Kitty Hawk, North Carolina? Crack this code by writing the letter of the alphabet that comes BEFORE each letter.

T H E   N A T I O N A L
U I F   O B U J P O B M

W E A T H E R   S E R V I C E
X F B U I F S   T F S W J D F

R E P O R T E D   T H A T
S F Q P S U F E   U I B U

I T   W A S   O N E   O F
J U   X B T   P O F   P G

T H E   W I N D I E S T
U I F   X J O E J F T U

S P O T S   I N   N O R T H
T Q P U T   J O   O P S U I

A M E R I C A.
B N F S J D B

For Sale

A website known as AuctionWeb first launched during Labor Day Weekend 1995. Today we know the site as eBay. What was the first item ever listed? Use this special code to decipher the answer.

```
A B C
D E I
K L M
```

N O P
Q R S
T U Y

A   B R O K E N

L A S E R

P O I N T E R

Largest Privately Owned U.S. Home

Built between 1889 and 1895 by George Washington Vanderbilt II, this French château-style mansion with 250 rooms is the largest privately owned home in the U.S. What is the name of this home and where is it located? Crack this code by writing the letter of the alphabet that comes BEFORE each letter.

THE BILTMORE
UIF CJMUNPSF

ESTATE NEAR
FTUBUF OFBS

ASHEVILLE,
BTIFWJMMF

NORTH
OPSUI

CAROLINA
DBSPMJOB

page 9

Lincoln's Tomb

Abraham Lincoln is not buried in the Lincoln Memorial. Where is our 16th president's tomb located? Decode the answer using this special code chart.

Symbol	= Letter
	= D
	= I
	= P
	= N
	= S
	= R
	= I
	= G
	= L
	= O
	= E
	= S
	= I
	= L
	= N
	= I
	= F
	= L
	= I

SPRINGFIELD,

ILLINOIS

page 10

Microwave Oven

How was the microwave oven accidentally invented? Cross out all the odd-numbered letters in this puzzle grid. List the remaining letters, in the order they appear, in the spaces below.

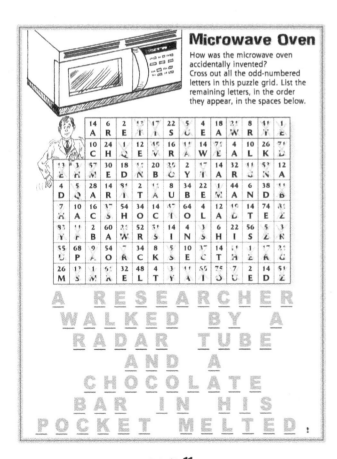

A RESEARCHER
WALKED BY A
RADAR TUBE
AND A
CHOCOLATE
BAR IN HIS
POCKET MELTED!

page 11

Miss Liberty's Crown

There are seven rays on the Statue of Liberty's crown, each measuring up to 9 feet in length and weighing as much as 150 pounds. What do the rays stand for? Decode the answer using the chart below.

A ●-	J ●---	S ●●●			
B -●●●	K -●-	T -			
C -●-●	L ●-●●	U ●●-			
D -●●	M --	V ●●●-			
E ●	N -●	W ●--			
F ●●-●	O ---	X -●●-			
G --●	P ●--●	Y -●--			
H ●●●●	Q --●-	Z --●●			
I ●●	R ●-●				

THE
- ●●●●

SEVEN
●●● ● ●●●- ● -●

CONTINENTS
-●-● --- -●- ●● -● ●● -● - ●●●

page 12

39

Mother, Wife & Cousin

Name the only person to be a mother, wife, and cousin to a U.S. President.

As you read each sentence below, decide whether the statement is true or false.

If the sentence is true, circle the letter under the TRUE column. If the sentence is false, circle the letter under the FALSE column. The circled letters, once listed below in the order they appear, will reveal the answer.

		TRUE	FALSE
1.	The city of Paris is located in France.	Ⓑ	A
2.	Valentine's Day is celebrated on February 14.	Ⓐ	E
3.	The first man walked on the moon in 1999.	C	Ⓡ
4.	George Washington had a pet dinosaur.	I	Ⓑ
5.	Albert Einstein owned the first Apple computer.	L	Ⓐ
6.	Bananas contain potassium.	Ⓡ	O
7.	Frogs can give you warts.	S	Ⓐ
8.	There are 30 days in November.	Ⓑ	T
9.	Benjamin Franklin invented bifocals.	Ⓤ	R
10.	Dragons existed during the Middle Ages.	E	Ⓢ
11.	Twelve inches equal one foot.	Ⓗ	Y

B A R B A R A   B U S H

page 13

No Election

This is the only man who held both the Presidency and the Vice-Presidency but who was not elected to either post. Discover his name by first drawing a line through these presidential words hidden in the puzzle below.

The letters that remain in the puzzle, once listed in the order they appear, will spell out the answer.

ADVISORS
CABINET
CAPITOL
CONGRESS
DEMOCRAT
LIMIT
OATH
OFFICE
REPUBLICAN
SENATE
STAFF
TERM

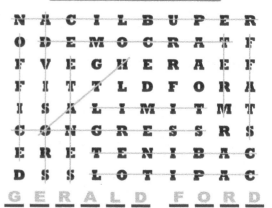

```
N A C I L B U P E R
O D E M O C R A T F
F V E G H E R A E F
F I T T L D F O R A
I S A L I M I T M T
C O N G R E S S R S
E R E T E N I B A C
D S S L O T I P A C
```

G E R A L D   F O R D

page 14

Now Hiring

What U.S. company currently employs more than 2 million people, making it the largest employer in America?

Darken in the areas that have a DOT ● to discover the answer.

page 15

Of Monumental Size

Opened in 1967 and standing 630 feet tall, this is the tallest man-made monument in the United States. Solve the secret code to find out what this is and where it can be found.

THE GATEWAY
ARCH IN
ST. LOUIS,
MISSOURI

page 16

Our Nation's Capital

Washington, D.C. is not a state. Named after President George Washington, what does the D.C. stand for? Decode and complete the answer.

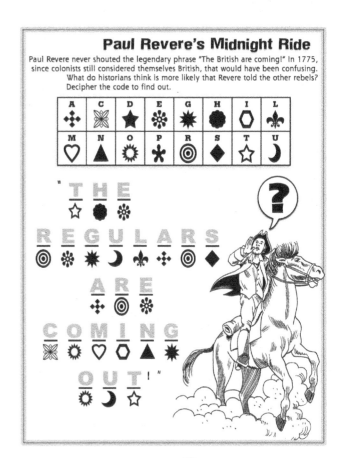

A	B	C	D	E	F	G	H	I	L
ny	ca	fl	nj	ct	vt	tx	nd	va	al

M	N	O	P	R	S	T	U	V	Y
co	ks	nv	ut	wy	ak	az	de	ga	ma

D I S T R I C T   O F
nj va ak az wy va fl az   nv vt

C O L U M B I A ,
fl nv al de co ca va ny

"DISTRICT" BECAUSE IT IS NOT PART OF A

S T A T E   A N D
ak az ny az ct   ny ks nj

"COLUMBIA" FOR

N A V I G A T O R
ks ny ga va tx ny az nv wy

C H R I S T O P H E R
fl nd wy va ak az nv ut nd ct wy

C O L U M B U S .
fl nv al de co ca de ak

Paul Revere's Midnight Ride

Paul Revere never shouted the legendary phrase "The British are coming!" In 1775, since colonists still considered themselves British, that would have been confusing. What do historians think is more likely that Revere told the other rebels? Decipher the code to find out.

"**T H E**

R E G U L A R S

A R E

C O M I N G

O U T !"

Peanuts?

Most of us call the main ingredient in peanut butter ... peanuts. But what do Georgia locals call them?
Write the name of each picture in its space. One letter from each word will spell out the answer.

H O T D O G

T O A S T E R

F R O G

B E D

H A M M E R

T R E E

S H O E

Pony Express

What state capital city was once the last stop for the Pony Express? Decipher the code to find out.

A	B	C	D	E	F	G	H	I	J	K	L	M

N	O	P	Q	R	S	T	U	V	W	X	Y	Z

S A C R A M E N T O ,

C A L I F O R N I A

Popular Children's Novel

What American novel, written by Louisa May Alcott, is about four sisters named Meg, Jo, Beth and Amy? Write the opposite of each word in the puzzle grid. One letter from each will spell out and decode the answer.

DROP	LIFT
TAKE	GIVE
STAND	SIT
CATCH	THROW
RIGHT	LEFT
TEACH	LEARN
STRONG	WEAK
SUNNY	CLOUDY
WOMAN	MAN
ENTER	EXIT
BEGIN	END

page 21

Presidential Portraits

Celebrated artist Norman Rockwell is known for his patriotic illustrations of American life. Rockwell painted portraits of only 4 U.S. presidents. The word PORTRAIT appears 7 times in this puzzle. Find and circle each one. The letters that remain, once listed below in the order they appear, will spell out the names of these four presidents.

```
P O R T R A I T E
O I S E N H O P T
R W E R K E O N I
T I A R T R O P A
R N E D T Y J O R
A P O R T R A I T
I H A N S O N A R
T I A R T R O P O
T N D N I X O N P
```

EISENHOWER, KENNEDY, JOHNSON AND NIXON

page 22

President's Airplane

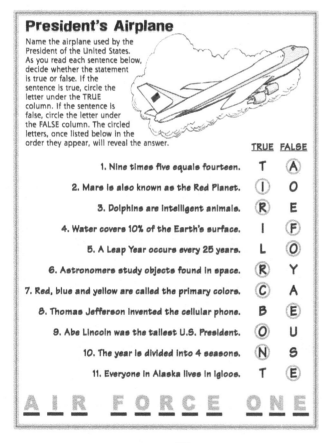

Name the airplane used by the President of the United States. As you read each sentence below, decide whether the statement is true or false. If the sentence is true, circle the letter under the TRUE column. If the sentence is false, circle the letter under the FALSE column. The circled letters, once listed below in the order they appear, will reveal the answer.

	TRUE	FALSE
1. Nine times five equals fourteen.	T	(A)
2. Mars is also known as the Red Planet.	(I)	O
3. Dolphins are intelligent animals.	(R)	E
4. Water covers 10% of the Earth's surface.	I	(F)
5. A Leap Year occurs every 25 years.	L	(O)
6. Astronomers study objects found in space.	(R)	Y
7. Red, blue and yellow are called the primary colors.	(C)	A
8. Thomas Jefferson invented the cellular phone.	B	(E)
9. Abe Lincoln was the tallest U.S. President.	(O)	U
10. The year is divided into 4 seasons.	(N)	S
11. Everyone in Alaska lives in igloos.	T	(E)

AIR FORCE ONE

page 23

"Satchmo"

Known around the world as "Satchmo," this cultural icon is widely recognized as a founding father of jazz. Who is this musician from New Orleans who helped make jazz famous with his trumpet and unique singing voice?

```
A E G H I L
M N O P R S
T U W X Y Z
```

LOUIS

ARMSTRONG

page 24

42

Secret Service

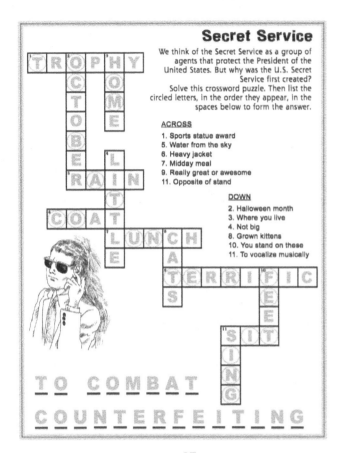

We think of the Secret Service as a group of agents that protect the President of the United States. But why was the U.S. Secret Service first created?
Solve this crossword puzzle. Then list the circled letters, in the order they appear, in the spaces below to form the answer.

ACROSS
1. Sports statue award
5. Water from the sky
6. Heavy jacket
7. Midday meal
9. Really great or awesome
11. Opposite of stand

DOWN
2. Halloween month
3. Where you live
4. Not big
8. Grown kittens
10. You stand on these
11. To vocalize musically

TO COMBAT COUNTERFEITING

page 25

Serving Others

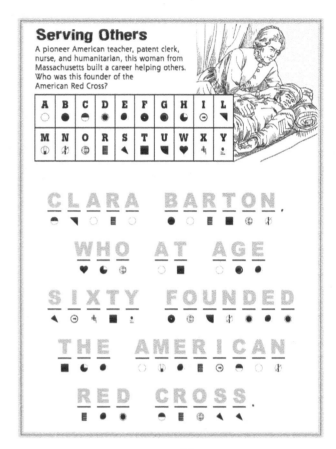

A pioneer American teacher, patent clerk, nurse, and humanitarian, this woman from Massachusetts built a career helping others. Who was this founder of the American Red Cross?

CLARA BARTON,
WHO AT AGE
SIXTY FOUNDED
THE AMERICAN
RED CROSS.

page 26

A Shocking Win

On August 24, 1919, Cleveland Indians pitcher Ray Caldwell completed a winning game against the Philadelphia Athletics. What was so unusual about this win? Cross out only the letters that contain this symbol ▦. The remaining letters, once listed below in the order they appear, will spell out the answer.

HE WAS STRUCK
BY LIGHTNING
IN THE MIDDLE
OF THE NINTH
INNING!

page 27

Shortest Inaugural Address

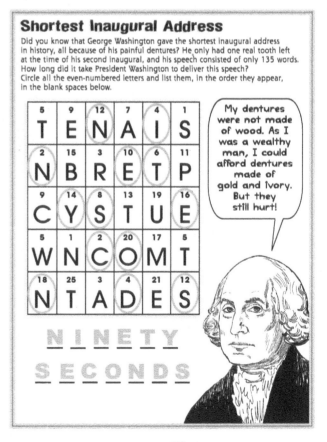

Did you know that George Washington gave the shortest inaugural address in history, all because of his painful dentures? He only had one real tooth left at the time of his second inaugural, and his speech consisted of only 135 words. How long did it take President Washington to deliver this speech?
Circle all the even-numbered letters and list them, in the order they appear, in the blank spaces below.

5	9	12	7	4	1
T	E	N	A	I	S

2	15	3	10	6	11
N	B	R	E	T	P

9	14	5	13	19	16
C	Y	S	T	U	E

5	1	20	2	17	5
W	N	C	O	M	T

18	25	3	4	21	12
N	T	A	D	E	S

NINETY SECONDS

My dentures were not made of wood. As I was a wealthy man, I could afford dentures made of gold and ivory. But they still hurt!

page 28

43

Shortest Presidency

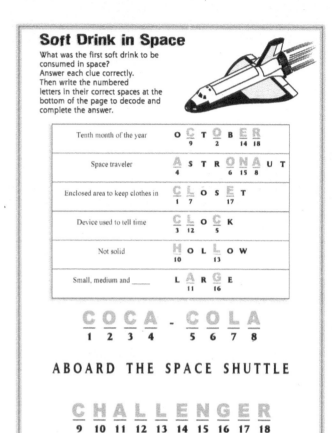

He gave the longest inaugural address in U.S. history, but had the shortest presidency. To decode his name, write the letter of the alphabet that comes BEFORE each letter.

W I L L I A M   H E N R Y
X J M M J B N   I F O S Z

H A R R I S O N,
I B S S J T P O

W H O
X I P

D I E D   J U S T
E J F E   K V T U

T H I R T Y - O N E
U I J S U Z   P O F

D A Y S   I N T O   H I S
E B Z T   J O U P   I J T

T E R M   F R O M
U F S N   G S P N

P N E U M O N I A.
Q O F V N P O J B

page 29

Soft Drink in Space

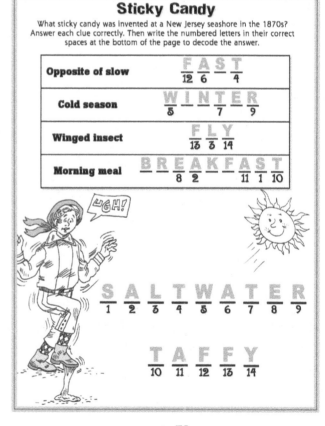

What was the first soft drink to be consumed in space? Answer each clue correctly. Then write the numbered letters in their correct spaces at the bottom of the page to decode and complete the answer.

Tenth month of the year	O C T O B E R
	9 2 14 18
Space traveler	A S T R O N A U T
	4 6 15 8
Enclosed area to keep clothes in	C L O S E T
	1 7 17
Device used to tell time	C L O C K
	3 12 5
Not solid	H O L L O W
	10 13
Small, medium and ____	L A R G E
	11 16

C O C A - C O L A
1 2 3 4   5 6 7 8

ABOARD THE SPACE SHUTTLE

C H A L L E N G E R
9 10 11 12 13 14 15 16 17 18

page 30

Special Delivery

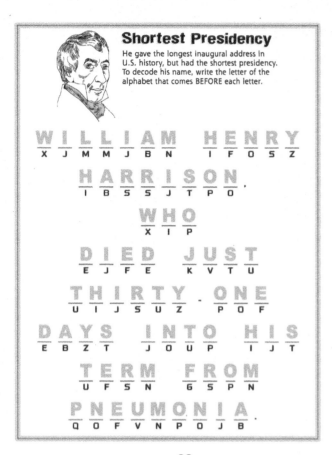

Where is the only place in the U.S. where mail is still delivered by mule?

MAIL'S HERE!

| A | B | C | D | E | F | G | H | I | L | M | N | O | P | R | S | T | U | V | Y |

H A V A S U P A I

L O C A T E D

A T   T H E

B O T T O M

O F   T H E

G R A N D

C A N Y O N !

page 31

Sticky Candy

What sticky candy was invented at a New Jersey seashore in the 1870s? Answer each clue correctly. Then write the numbered letters in their correct spaces at the bottom of the page to decode the answer.

Opposite of slow	F A S T
	12 6 4
Cold season	W I N T E R
	5 7 9
Winged insect	F L Y
	13 3 14
Morning meal	B R E A K F A S T
	8 2 11 1 10

UGH!

S A L T W A T E R
1 2 3 4 5 6 7 8 9

T A F F Y
10 11 12 13 14

page 32

44